SEEKING A PURER CHRISTIAN LIFE

Sayings and Stories of the
DESERT FATHERS
AND MOTHERS

Upper Room Spiritual Classics® — Series 3

D0907999

Selected, edited, and introduced by
Keith Beasley-Topliffe

UPPER
ROOM BOOKS™
NASHVILLE

Seeking a Purer Christian Life:
Saying and Stories of the Desert Mothers and Fathers

Copyright © 2000 by Upper Room Books™
All rights reserved.

The Upper Room® Website: http://www.upperroom.org

Scripture quotations are from the New Revised Standard Version of the Bible Copyright © 1989 by the Division of Christian Education of the National Council of Churches of Christ in the USA. Used by permission. All rights reserved.

Excerpts from *The World of the Desert Fathers* by Columba Stewart OSB, 1986, are printed by permission of SLG Press, Convent of the Incarnation. Fairacres, Oxford, England. Sisters of the Love of God.

Excerpts from *Harlots of the Desert* by Benedicta Ward SLG, 1987. Published by Cistercian Publications, Kalamazoo, Michigan 49008.

Cover design: Gore Studio, Inc.
Interior design and layout: Nancy J. Cole

First printing: 2000

Library of Congress Cataloging-in-Publication Data

Seeking a purer Christian life : sayings and stories of the Desert
    Fathers and Mothers / selected, edited, and introduced by Keith
    Beasley-Topliffe.
        p. cm. — (Upper Room spiritual classics. Series 3)
    ISBN 0-8358-0902-1
        1. Desert Fathers Quotations. 2. Spiritual life—Christianity
Quotations, maxims, etc. I. Beasley-Topliffe, Keith. II. Series.
BR63.S44 2000   99-37907
270.2—dc21   CIP

Printed in the United States of America

TABLE OF CONTENTS

INTRODUCTION

What does it take to lead a Christian life? Would a simpler lifestyle help us learn detachment from the things of this world? Would getting away from the distractions of our lives make us holier?

In the third, fourth, and fifth centuries, thousands of men and women abandoned the cities of the eastern Mediterranean to seek simplicity, solitude, and Christian community in the deserts of Egypt and Syria. Some lived alone, seeing others only at daily or weekly services of worship. Some lived in communities of thousands, working and worshiping together. They learned that fleeing external distractions only brought them face-to-face with the root of temptation in their own thoughts—the demons of lust, greed, pride, and envy were still with them. They also learned about the depths of God's mercy and forgiveness and the power of the Holy Spirit to overcome every other spirit and cleanse the soul.

Though the desert dwellers rarely wrote anything, others began to tell stories about them: how they came to repentance, how they fought against temptation, how they lived in community. They also wrote the teachings of the desert mothers and fathers, sometimes arranged in long speeches, sometimes only a few words of wisdom. Through these writings, desert teachings about prayer, spiritual disciplines, and living together spread throughout the Christian world and became the foundation of monasticism in

Western Europe as well as in the Eastern Church. The following selections include both stories and sayings illustrating the wisdom of the desert.

THE WORLD OF THE DESERT

When Anthony, the first of the desert fathers, journeyed into the desert around A.D. 285, the Roman Empire still controlled all the area around the Mediterranean Sea. Though frequently torn by war between rival emperors, the empire provided a common culture in which Christianity grew despite persecution. By the late third century, Christianity was often tolerated even though officially illegal. Christians were able to build large churches in many cities. In 303, however, Emperor Diocletian attempted to restore Rome's power through strict adherence to the Roman gods. Many Christians were imprisoned or killed. Others denied Christ and sacrificed to the gods of Rome.

After Diocletian's death, one of the rivals competing for power became a Christian. Constantine saw in a dream that he could win if his banners displayed the sign of the cross. After his victory, he first declared toleration for all religions, then made Christianity the official religion of the empire. Suddenly bishops had secular as well as spiritual power, and only Christians could hope for advancement in government service.

Constantine soon discovered that the faith he had embraced and promoted was split in many factions. Debate raged over doctrinal issues such as the nature of Christ and his relation to God the Father and over practical questions such as what to do about Christians who had fallen away during persecution and now wished to return. Convinced that only a united church could unite the empire, he called a council in Niceaa (325) to decide these matters, and he offered the might of the empire to enforce its decisions.

These changes in the church and the world provided several motives for men and women to go into the desert. Some may have become disgusted with the secularization of Christianity, believing that it had become so easy to be a Christian that few took spiritual disciplines seriously. Others may have sought a refuge from the controversies, a place where living a Christian life was more important than debating fine points of doctrine. The desert offered opportunities for harsh discipline and hard work, solitude for prayer, space to form new kinds of communities dedicated to Christian living.

LIFE IN THE DESERT

Anthony, first of the fathers, was born about 251 in Egypt in a Christian family. His parents died when he was about eighteen. He then sold his estate, placed his sister with a community of women, and began to seek spiritual guidance from older men in the area. He lived outside his home village for some time, then (about 285) lived alone in an abandoned fort in the mountains just east of the Nile for about twenty years. Many people came to seek his wisdom and some stayed nearby as disciples. He returned to Alexandria briefly during the Diocletian persecution, then returned to the desert to organize his followers into a slightly more structured community. About 313 he went farther into the desert to a mountain near the Red Sea. He lived there until his death in 356 at the age of 105. His friend Athanasius, bishop of Alexandria, wrote a book of Anthony's life the next year. It was quickly translated into several languages and spread throughout the empire. Reading the *Life of Anthony* was a key ingredient in the conversion of Augustine ten years later.

Meanwhile, many others had followed Anthony into the desert on both sides of the Nile in central Egypt (the Thebaid). About 320, Pachomius founded a community in Tabennisi in Upper Egypt (that is, upstream farther south). His leadership was chronicled in the *Rule of Pachomius*. Other communities grew in the salt marshes of the Nile Delta and in the desert east of Jerusalem in Syria.

Soon there were three basic forms of desert life. A few were solitaries like Anthony, though their solitude was often interrupted by visitors or ended as communities of disciples grew up around them. Some lived in clusters of separate huts or cells, close enough to permit worship and guidance in common while still preserving solitude most of the time. Most (including almost all the women) lived in highly structured communities like that of Pachomius. Thousands resided in some of these communities.

The primary work of these desert dwellers was prayer. Prayer was supposed to be constant, whatever else the monk or nun might be doing. Some monks made baskets or ropes to support themselves. Others hired out as farm laborers. Some, who carried on ministries of spiritual direction (including leadership of communities), were given the title Amma (Mother) or Abba (Father).

By the end of the fourth century the desert was filled with tens of thousands of men and women. People came from long distances to learn from the wisest. Palladius visited Egypt in 388 and wrote a history of the monks for his friend Lausus (and so called the *Lausiac History*) thirty years later. In 385 their monastery in Jerusalem sent John Cassian and his companion to visit the most famous fathers and bring back a report. Much later Cassian moved to southern France where he wrote *Institutes* and *Conferences*, interpreting the desert life for monastic communities in Western Europe. In 394, another group of tourist monks from Jerusalem visited Egypt. Ten years later one of them wrote *History of the Monks in Egypt*, an account of the trip. Meanwhile collections of sayings of various fathers (and some mothers too) were written down and collected. Many sayings include a brief story to provide context.

By the beginning of the fifth century, with Roman power declining, the desert became unsafe. Bands of raiders swept in from the desert to devastate monasteries and other communities. Many monks moved to safer areas. Others stayed and were killed. The era of Egyptian monasticism was over.

FURTHER READING

There have been several modern translations of the sayings and stories of the desert. Most notable is a series of translations by Benedicta Ward and various collaborators. These include *The Sayings of the Desert Fathers*, *The Lives of the Desert Fathers* (a translation of *History of the Monks in Egypt*), and *Harlots of the Desert*—all available from Cistercian Publications—as well as *The World of the Desert Fathers* and *The Wisdom of the Desert Fathers* from SLG Press. All of them are very readable and contain excellent introductions. A few of the sayings were translated and introduced by Thomas Merton in *The Wisdom of the Desert* (New Directions). Paulist Press has published selections from John Cassian's *Conferences* as well as a translation of the *Life of Anthony* by Athanasius. Modern translations of the *Lausiac History* and *Rule of Pachomius* are less readily available.

The traditions of desert spirituality were carried forward in the Eastern Church by many writers. Much of their wisdom is anthologized in the *Philokalia*, available in English translation in several volumes from Faber and Faber. In the Western Church, the *Rule of St. Benedict* (available in many translations) set the standard for Western monasticism.

NOTE ON THE TEXT

Selections from the *Life of Anthony* are from the translation in the *Nicene and Post-Nicene Fathers*, Series 2. The story of Maria and Abraham is from Benedicta Ward's translation of an early Latin version in *Harlots of the Desert*. Selections from the *Lausiac History* and *History of the Monks in Egypt* are from Ernest A. Wallis Budge's translation of a Syriac anthology of monastic sources called *The Paradise of the Fathers*. Selections from *Sayings of the Fathers* are from Benedicta Ward's translation of the "alphabetical collection" in *The Sayings of the Desert Fathers* except for the stories of the two wise women from *The World of the Desert Fathers*, translated by Columba Stewart.

All selections have been edited for length and inclusive language. Grammar, punctuation, and spelling have been modernized and Americanized. The older translations have required more extensive modernization. Where possible, scriptural quotes have been conformed to the New Revised Standard Version.

ANTHONY'S BEGINNINGS IN DISCIPLINE

From *Life of Anthony*, Chapters 1–4

Athanasius, bishop of Alexandria wrote The Life of Anthony in 357, the year after Anthony's death. He knew Anthony personally and received the testimony of others. This selection begins the story.

You should know that Anthony was an Egyptian by descent. His parents were of good family and possessed considerable wealth. Since they were Christians, he also was reared in that faith. In infancy he was brought up with his parents, knowing nothing else but them and his home. But when he was grown to boyhood and was advancing in years, he could not stand to learn letters or to associate with other boys. All his desire was, as it is written of Jacob, to live as "a quiet man" at home. He used to attend the Lord's house with his parents. He was not idle as a child nor did he despise his parents when older. He was obedient to his father and mother and attentive to what was read, keeping in his heart what was profitable in what he heard. Though as a child he was brought up in moderate affluence, he did not trouble his parents for varied or luxurious fare, nor was this a source of pleasure to him. He was content simply with what he found and did not seek anything further.

After the deaths of his father and mother he was left alone with one little sister. He was about eighteen or twenty, and the care of both home and sister rested on him. Not six months after the deaths of his parents, he went according to custom into the Lord's house. As he walked, he communed with himself and reflected how the apostles left all and followed the Savior, and how, in Acts, people sold their possessions and brought and laid them at the apostles' feet for distribution to the needy, and how great a hope was laid up for them in heaven. Pondering these things, he entered the church. It happened that the Gospel was being read, and he heard the Lord saying to the rich man, "If you wish to be perfect, go, sell your possessions, and give the money to the poor, and you will have treasure in heaven; then come, follow me." Anthony went out immediately from the church, as though God had put him in mind of the saints and the passage had been read on his account. He gave the possessions of his ancestors to the villagers—they were three hundred acres, productive and very fair—that they should be no more a clog upon himself and his sister. All the rest that was movable he sold. Having got together much money, he gave it to the poor, reserving just a little for his sister's sake.

He went again into the church and heard the Lord say in the Gospel, "Do not worry about tomorrow." He could stay no longer but went out and gave those things also to the poor. He committed his sister to known and faithful virgins and put her into a convent to be brought up. From then on, he devoted himself outside his house to discipline, watching over himself and training himself with patience. There were not yet many monasteries in Egypt, and no monk at all knew of the distant desert. All who wished to watch over themselves practiced the discipline in solitude near their own villages.

There was an old man then in the next village who had lived the life of a hermit from his youth. After he had seen this man, Anthony imitated him in piety. At first he lived in places outside the village. Then if he heard of a good man anywhere, he went forth like the prudent bee and sought him, not returning to his own place until he had seen him and gotten from the good man supplies for his journey in the way of virtue. So by dwelling there at first, he confirmed his purpose not to return to his ancestral home or to the remembrance of his kinsfolk.

Anthony kept all his desire and energy for perfecting his discipline. He worked with his hands since he had heard, "Anyone unwilling to work should not eat." He spent part on bread and gave part to the needy. He was constant in prayer, knowing that people ought to pray in secret unceasingly. He paid such attention to what was read that none of the things that were written fell from him to the ground. He remembered all, and afterward his memory served him for books.

While he lived in that way, Anthony was loved by all. He subjected himself in sincerity to the good men whom he visited and learned thoroughly where each surpassed him in zeal and discipline. He observed the graciousness of one and the unceasing prayer of another. He learned from another's freedom from anger and another's loving-kindness. He paid attention to one as he watched and to another as he studied. He admired one for his endurance and another for his fasting and sleeping on the ground. He watched carefully the meekness of one and the long-suffering of another and noted the piety toward Christ and the mutual love that animated all. He returned to his own place of discipline filled with these things and then strove to unite the qualities of each. He was eager to show in himself the virtues of all. He had no rivalry with others of the same age except this: that he should not be second to them in higher things. He did this in a way that hurt nobody's feelings, but made them rejoice over him. So all the people of that village and the good men he spoke with intimately, when they saw that he was a man of this sort, would call him God-beloved. Some welcomed him as a son, others as a brother.

ANThONY'S STRUGGLE

From *Life of Anthony*, Chapters 12–14

After several years of disciplined living near his home, Anthony wanted more solitude. He went south into the desert between the Nile and the Red Sea. He was about thirty-five years old.

More and more confirmed in his purpose, Anthony hurried to the mountain. He found a fort, so long deserted that it was full of creeping things, on the other side of the river. He crossed over to it and dwelled there. The reptiles immediately left the place, as though someone were chasing them. He sealed up the entrance completely, having stored up loaves for six months—it is a custom of the Thebans, and the loaves often remain fresh a whole year. Since he found water inside, he could stay inside by himself, never going out or looking at anyone who came. Thus he spent a long time training himself, and received loaves, let down from above, twice a year.

But those of his acquaintances who came often used to spend days and nights outside since he did not permit them to enter. They heard something like crowds inside, making noises and crying with piteous voices, "Go from what is ours. What are you doing in the desert? You cannot withstand our attack." So at first those outside thought that there were some men fighting with him, and that they had entered by ladders. But when they stooped down, they saw through a hole there was nobody. They were afraid, figuring it was demons, and they called on Anthony. He heard them quickly, though he had not given a thought to the demons. Coming to the door, he asked them to leave and not to be afraid, He said, "The demons seem to make attacks against those who are cowardly. Sign yourselves therefore with the cross and depart boldly. Let them make sport for themselves." So they departed fortified with the sign of the cross.

But Anthony remained completely unharmed by the evil spirits. Nor was he wearied with the contest, for visions from above came to his aid, and the weakness of the foe relieved him of much trouble and armed him with greater zeal. His acquaintances would often come expecting to find him dead and would hear him singing, "Let God rise up. Let his enemies be scattered; let those who hate him flee before him. As smoke is driven away, so drive them away; as wax melts before the fire, let the wicked perish before God." And again, "All nations surrounded me; in the name of the Lord I cut them off!"

And so for nearly twenty years, he continued training himself in solitude, never going forth, and but seldom seen by any. After this many eagerly wanted to imitate his discipline, and his acquaintances came and began to cast down and wrench off the door by force. Anthony, as from a shrine, came forth initiated in the mysteries and filled with the Spirit of God.

Then for the first time he was seen outside the fort by those who came to see him. When they saw him, they wondered at the sight, for his body was in the same shape as before and was neither fat like a man without exercise nor lean from fasting and striving with the demons. He was just the same as they had known him before his retirement. His soul was still free from blemish, neither contracted as if by grief nor relaxed by pleasure nor possessed by laughter or dejection, for he was not troubled when he beheld the crowd or overjoyed at being saluted by so many.

Through him the Lord healed the bodily illnesses of many present and cleansed others from evil spirits. God gave grace to Anthony in speaking so that he consoled many who were sorrowful and united those who had differences, exhorting all to prefer the love of Christ before all that is in the world. And while he exhorted and advised them to remember the good things to come and the loving-kindness toward us of God, "who did not withhold his own Son, but gave him up for all of us," he persuaded many to embrace the solitary life. And so it happened in the end that cells arose even in the mountains, and the desert was colonized by monks who came forth from their own people and enrolled themselves for citizenship in the heavens.

ANTHONY'S TESTIMONY

From *Life of Anthony*, Chapters 39–42

After coming out from his cell, Anthony began to speak about struggling against temptations and demonic attacks. In this selection he concludes the discourse with some of his experiences.

How often have the evil spirits called me blessed, and I have cursed them in the name of the Lord! How often have they predicted the rising of the river, and I answered them, "What have you to do with it?" Once they came threatening and surrounded me like soldiers in full armor. At another time they filled the house with horses, wild beasts, and creeping things. But I sang, "Some take pride in chariots, and some in horses, but our pride is in the name of the Lord our God," and they were turned to flight by the Lord. Once they came in darkness, bearing the appearance of a light, and said, "We came to give you a light, Anthony." But I closed my eyes and prayed. Immediately the light of the wicked ones was quenched. A few months later they came as though singing psalms and babbling the words of Scripture. "But I am like the deaf. I do not hear." Once they shook the cell with an earthquake, but I continued praying with unshaken heart. And after that, they came again making noises, whistling, and dancing. But as I prayed and lay singing psalms to myself, they immediately began to lament and weep as if their strength had failed them. But I gave glory to the Lord who had brought them down and made an example of their daring and madness.

Once a very tall demon appeared with pomp and dared to say, "I am the power of God and I am Providence. What do you want me to give you?" But I then breathed on him and spoke the name of Christ and prepared to hit him. And I seemed to have hit him, and at once, big as he was, he and all his demons disappeared at the name of Christ. At another time while I was fasting, he came full of craft, under the semblance of a monk with what seemed to be loaves and advised me, "Eat and cease from all your labors. You also are a man and likely to fall sick." But I, perceiving his trick, rose up to pray. He could not endure it, for he departed and seemed to go through the door like smoke. Often they would beat me, and I repeated again and again, "Nothing shall separate me from the love of Christ." At that they fell to beating one another. But it was not I who stopped them and destroyed their power: it was the Lord, who said, "I watched Satan fall from heaven like a flash of lightning." But, children, in the Apostle's words, "I have applied all this to myself," that you might learn not to faint in discipline or to fear the devil or the delusions of the demons.

And since I have become a fool in describing these things, receive this also as an aid to your safety and fearlessness. Believe me, for I do not lie. Once someone knocked at the door of my cell. When I went out, I saw one who seemed of great size and tall. Then when I asked, "Who are you?" he said, "I am Satan." Then when I said, "Why are you here?" he answered, "Why do the monks and all other Christians blame me undeservedly? Why do they curse me hourly?" Then I answered, "Why do you trouble them?" He said, "I am not the one who troubles them. They trouble themselves, for I have become weak. Have they not read, 'The enemies have vanished in everlasting ruins; their cities you have rooted out'? I no longer have a place, a weapon, a city. The Christians are spread everywhere, and at length even the desert is filled with monks. They should look after themselves and not curse me unreservedly." Then I marveled at the grace of the Lord and said to him: "You are always a liar and never speak the truth. But at least you have spoken this truly, even if against your will, for the coming of Christ has made you weak. He has cast you down and stripped you." But when he heard the Savior's name, he could not bear the burning from it and vanished.

If, therefore, the devil himself confesses that his power is gone, we ought utterly to despise both him and his demons. Since the enemy with his hounds has tricks only of this sort, we—now that we know their weakness—are able to despise them. So let us not despair or have a thought of cowardice in our hearts or frame fears for ourselves, saying, I am afraid a demon might come and overthrow me or lift me up and cast me down or confound me by rising against me suddenly. Let us not have such thoughts in mind at all or be sorrowful as though we were perishing. Rather let us be courageous and rejoice always, believing that we are safe. Let us consider in our souls that the Lord who is with us put the evil spirits to flight and broke their power. Let us consider and take to heart that while the Lord is with us, our foes can do us no harm. For when they come, they approach us in a form corresponding to the state in which they discover us and adapt their delusions to the condition of mind in which they find us. If, therefore, they find us timid and confused, they at once attack like robbers, having found our minds unguarded. Whatever we are thinking about, they do—and more also. For if they find us fainthearted and cowardly, they greatly increase our terror by their delusions and threats. But if they see us rejoicing in the Lord, contemplating the bliss of the future, mindful of the Lord, considering that all things are in God's hand and that no evil spirit has any strength against the Christian or any power at all over anyone—if they behold the soul fortified with these thoughts—they are baffled and turned backward.

ANThONY'S ADVICE

From *Life of Anthony*, Chapters 55–56, 58

After a brief return to the city to encourage Christians suffering persecution, Anthony returned to the desert, going even father into the wilderness. Even there people followed him, some building cells near his, others simply asking advice. Here is some of the guidance he offered.

"Believe in the Lord and love him. Keep yourselves from impure thoughts and fleshly pleasures. Pray continually. Avoid vanity. Sing psalms before sleep and on awaking. Hold in your heart the commandments of Scripture. Be mindful of the works of the saints so that your souls, being put in remembrance of the commandments, may be brought into harmony with the zeal of the saints."

He especially counseled them to meditate continually on the Apostle's word, "Do not let the sun go down on your anger." He considered this was spoken of all commandments in common and that not on anger alone, but not on any other sin of ours ought the sun to go down. He said, "It is good and needful that neither should the sun condemn us for an evil by day nor the moon for a sin by night or even for an evil thought. So that this state may be preserved in us, it is good to hear the Apostle and keep his words, for he says, 'Examine yourselves and test yourselves.' Daily,

therefore, let all take an account of their actions both
by day and by night. And if they have sinned, let
them cease from it. If they have not, let them not be
boastful but abide in what is good without being neg-
ligent or condemning their neighbors or justifying
themselves, 'until the Lord comes, who will bring to
light the things now hidden,' as the blessed apostle
Paul says. For often we do things unawares that we
do not know. But the Lord sees all things. So let us
have sympathy for one another and commit the judgment to God. Let us bear one another's burdens. But
let us examine ourselves and hasten to fill up whatever is lacking. As a safeguard against sin, let the following be observed. Let us each one note and write
down our actions and the impulses of our soul as
though we were going to relate them to one another.
Be assured that if we would be utterly ashamed to
have them known, we will abstain from sin and harbor
no base thoughts in our minds. For who wishes to be
seen while sinning? Who will not lie after the commis-
sion of a sin, through the wish to escape notice? As
we would not commit carnal sin while we are looking
at one another, so if we record our thoughts as though
about to tell them to one another, we shall more easily
keep ourselves free from vile thoughts through shame.
So let what we write take the place of the eyes of our
fellow hermits. Then blushing as much to write as if
we had been caught, we may never think of what is
unseemly. Thus forming ourselves, we shall be able to

keep the body in subjection, to please the Lord, and to trample on the tricks of the enemy."

This was the advice he gave to those who came to him. And with those who suffered he sympathized and prayed. And often the Lord heard him on behalf of many. Yet he did not boast because he was heard or complain if not. But always he gave the Lord thanks and asked the sufferer to be patient and know that healing belonged neither to him nor to any human, but only to the Lord, who does good when and to whom he will. The sufferers therefore used to receive the words of the old man as though they were a cure, learning not to be downhearted but to endure patiently. And those who were healed were taught to give thanks to not Anthony but to God alone.

There was also a maiden from Busiris Tripolitana, who had a terrible and very hideous disorder. For what ran from her eyes, nose, and ears fell to the ground and immediately became worms. She was paralyzed also and squinted. Her parents had heard of monks going to Anthony and believed in the Lord who healed the woman with the issue of blood. So they asked to be allowed, together with their daughter, to journey with them. And when they let them, the parents and the girl remained outside the mountain with Paphnutius, the confessor and monk. But the monks went in to Anthony. And when they were almost ready to tell about the damsel, he anticipated them and detailed the sufferings of the child and how she journeyed with them. Then they asked that she should be admitted. Anthony did not allow it, but said, "Go, and if she is not dead, you will find her healed. For the accomplishment of this is not mine, that she should come to me, wretched man that I am, but her healing is the work of the Savior, who in every place shows pity to those who call upon him. So the Lord has inclined to her as she prayed, and his loving-kindness has declared to me that he will heal the child where she now is." So the wonder took place. When the monks went out, they found the parents rejoicing and the girl whole.

Maria and Abraham

From *Life of Maria the Harlot* by Archdeacon Ephraim

Stories of repentance were popular among the desert monks, especially repentance of flagrant sinners such as murderers, thieves, and prostitutes. This story was written down by Ephraim, a disciple of Abraham and so personally acquainted with the details. Maria was an orphan whose uncle Abraham took her to the desert to live in a small room built onto his own hut. There she grew up, praying and learning the Scriptures. When she was seduced by a monk, she felt she was ruined and ran to the city to become a prostitute. It took Abraham two years to learn where she was.

Abraham put on the dress of a soldier and put a large hat on his head so that it hid his face, and he opened the door of his cell. He took with him a pound's weight in coins, and getting on the horse, he hastened away. He went through the countryside to the city, adopting the customs of the inhabitants so that he might not be recognized. Thus blessed Abraham made use of an alien dress that he might turn her back from her flight. Let us marvel at this second Abraham, for as the first Abraham went into battle with the kings and brought out his nephew, Lot, so this second Abraham went to war with the devil so that he might overcome him and bring back his niece with even more triumph.

When he reached the place, he wanted to arrange to see her with the least possible interruption, so he went up to the brothel-keeper and smiled, saying, "My friend, I hear that you have a very good girl indeed here. If I may, I would very much like to have her." The brothel-keeper said, "As you say, I have one who is beautiful beyond the usual run. Her beauty excels everything that nature can create." The old man then asked her name, and she replied that she was called Maria. Smiling with joy, Abraham then said, "I beg you to take me into her presence so that I may enjoy her today, for I have heard this girl praised by many." When the brothel-keeper heard this, she summoned Maria. When her uncle saw her in the dress of a harlot, he was almost overcome by grief. He had to hold back his tears by force, lest the brothel-keeper should know him and make him leave the courtyard.

When they had rested and drunk a little, this amazing man began to fondle her. He got up and put his arm around her neck and stroked it with his lips. When his lips touched her, Maria smelled the sweet smell of asceticism coming from his body, and she remembered the days when she, too, had lived as an ascetic. As if pierced by a spear, she cried out from her heart and burst into tears, unable to bear it; and she said as if to herself, "Alas, alas, how desolate I am!" The brothel-keeper was angry when she noticed this and said in surprise, "Whatever is the matter with you, Mistress Maria? You have been here for two

years and never before have I had word of complaint
from you." Maria said to her, "It would be better for
me if I could die before the third year has passed."
At that, the blessed old man was afraid she would rec-
ognize him, so he said soothingly to her, "If you go
on thinking about your sins, how can we expect to
enjoy ourselves?"

Then the holy man offered the brothel-keeper
the money he had brought and said to her, "My
friend, I want you to make us a very good meal so
that I may have this girl now. I have come a very long
way out of love for her." Forty years of abstinence
when he tasted nothing but bread, and now without
hesitation he chewed meat to save a soul from hell!
The choir of holy angels rejoiced and was amazed at
his discretion, for without hesitation he ate and drank
in order that he might draw a soul out of the mire!
Wisdom of wisdom, how this man, wise, discreet and
prudent, seemed a fool and indiscreet so that he might
snatch from the mouth of the lion the soul it had eaten
and set free from the darkness and bonds of sin the
soul that had been taken and bound!

When they had eaten, the girl drew Abraham to
the bed to lie down and took him toward the inner
chamber, and he said, "Let us go in." When he got
inside, he saw the bed set on a platform, and he
seated himself on it, as if eagerly. (What shall I say of
you, athlete of Christ? After forty years of conversion, you lie down on a prostitute's bed and wait for

her to come to you! All this you did for the praise and glory of Christ in order to save that lost soul.)

When he had seated himself on the bed, Maria said to him, "Come, sir, let me unfasten your trousers for you." And he said, "First close the door carefully and lock it." When she had locked the door, she came toward him, and the old man said to her, "Mistress Maria, come close to me." And when she had come close, he held her firmly with one hand, as if about to kiss her, but snatching the hat from his head, in a voice breaking with tears, he said to her, "Don't you know me, Maria, my child? Dear heart, am I not he who took care of you? Who hurt you, my daughter? What has become of your virginity, your tears, your vigils, all your prayers? From what a height you have fallen, my child, into such a pit as this! Why, when you sinned, did you not tell me? Why could you not come and speak of it with me? For of course I would have done penance for you. Why instead did you hurt me and give me this unbearable weight of grief? For who is without sin, save God alone?" While he was saying this and much besides, Maria sat like a stone between his hands, overcome both by shame and by fear. In tears, the old man said to her, "Why do you not speak to me, my heart? Have I not come to take you home, my child?" And so until the middle of the night Abraham consoled Maria with words of this kind and covered her with tears. After a while she plucked up courage, and weeping, she said to him, "I could not come to you; I was so very much ashamed. How can I pray again to God when I am defiled with sin as filthy as this?" The holy man said to her, "Upon me be your sin, Maria, and let God lay it to my account. Only listen to me and come, let us go back where we belong. My dear, do not draw back from the mercy of God. To you, your sins seem like mountains, but God has spread mercy over all that God has made. So we once read together how an unclean woman came to the Lord, and he did not send her away but cleansed her. And she washed his feet with her tears and wiped them with the hairs of her head. If spark could set fire to the ocean, then indeed your sins could defile the purity of God! It is not new to fall, my daughter. What is wrong is to lie down when you have fallen. Remember where you stood before you fell. The devil once mocked you, but now he will know that you can rise more strong than ever before. I beg you, take pity on my old age, and do not make me grieve any more. Get up, and come with me to our cell. Do not be afraid. Sin is only part of being human. It happened to you very quickly, and now by the help of God you are coming out of it even more quickly, for God does not will the death of sinners, but that they may live." Then she said to him, "If you know of any penance I can do that God will receive from me, command me and I will do it." So she laid her head on his feet and wept away the rest of the night, saying, "What shall I return to the Lord for all his bounty to me?"

When morning came, blessed Abraham said to her, "Get up, my daughter, and let us go home." She said to him, "I have this small amount of gold and these clothes. What do you want me to do with them?" And Abraham said, "Leave it all here, Maria, for it came from evil." So they got up and went out. He placed her on the horse, and he went first leading it, like a shepherd with the lost sheep he had found, bearing it home upon his shoulders with joy.

TWO WISE WOMEN

From *The Sayings of the Fathers*

For many monks, the strongest temptations for breaking their vows and leaving the desert were sexual. Here are two stories of women who, by refusing lustful men, helped them to overcome temptation and live holy lives.

A brother was sent on an errand by his abbot. Arriving at a place that had water, he found a woman there washing clothes. Overcome, he asked her if he might sleep with her. She said to him, "Listening to you is easy, but I could be the cause of great suffering for you." He said to her, "How?" She answered, "After committing the deed, your conscience will strike you, and either you will give up on yourself, or it will require great effort for you to reach the state that is yours now. Therefore, before you experience that hurt, go on your way in peace." When he heard this, he was struck with contrition and thanked both God and her wisdom. He went to his abbot, informed him of the event, and he, too, marveled. And the brother urged the rest not to go out of the monastery, and so he himself remained in the monastery, not going out until death.

—

There were two traders from Apamea in Syria who were friends and who traded abroad. One was wealthy, and the other was of moderate fortune. The wealthy man had a wife who was beautiful and also chaste, as events would prove. For when her husband died and the other man saw her worthiness, he wanted to take her to himself as his wife. But he was hesitant to speak to her, for fear that she would not accept. She was wise and knew what was going on and said to him, "Master Simeon"—for this was his name—"I see that you are thinking about something. Tell me what you feel and I will reassure you." At first he was hesitant to speak, but later he confessed to her and pleaded with her to become his wife. She said to him, "If you do what I command you, I will accept." He said to her, "Whatever you command me, I will do." She said to him, "Go into your workshop and fast until I summon you, and in truth I will not eat anything until I call for you." He agreed, but she did not tell him a specific time when she would call for him.

He went off for one day, then a second, then a third, and still she did not call for him. But he persevered, either because of love for her or because God had arranged matters and provided him with endurance, having seen where God was going to call him—for after all this he became a vessel of election. On the fourth day, she sent for him. He had little strength. Being unable to come on foot due to his suffering, he had to be carried. She for her part prepared a table and a bed and said to him, "Look, here is a table and there is a bed. Where do you wish to begin?" He said to her, "I implore you, have mercy on me and give me a bit to eat because I am weak. For if it were to be a woman first, I would not be capable of it due to the feebleness afflicting me." Then she said to him, "See you when you were hungry you preferred food to me, to every woman, and to pleasure? Therefore, whenever you have such thoughts, make use of this medicine and be free from every foul thought. For you have convinced me that after my husband, I shall marry neither you nor any other. But under the protection of Christ I hope to remain as I am, a widow." Then struck with contrition and marveling at her wisdom and self-restraint, he said to her, "Since the Lord has seen fit to oversee my salvation by means of your wisdom, what do you advise me to do?" She, moved by his youth and beauty, and being careful lest at that moment she also might suffer such a temptation, said to him, "By God, I believe that you love no one more than me." He said to her, "It is so." She said to him, "I, and this is God's truth, also love you, but since it is the voice of the Lord that says, 'Whoever comes to me and does not hate father and mother, wife and children, brothers and sisters, yes, and even life itself, cannot be my disciple,' let us part from each other because of God, so that the Lord might consider you to have renounced your wife because of God, and me to have renounced my husband. For there is a monastery of hermits in our region at Apamea, and if you are fully intending to be saved, become a monk there and you will truly please God." Immediately he gave up his trade, hastened to that monastery, and remained there until the time of his death. And he was esteemed, for he had a clean mind. He saw things in a suitable manner and regarded them spiritually.

 MARIA THE MONK

From the *Lausiac History of Palladius*

About 420, Palladius wrote a collection of stories about the desert for his patron, Lausus. Palladius may have titled the book Paradise, but it has come to be known as the Lausiac History. The monks believed that it was better to suffer false accusations and attacks in silence rather than accuse another of lying. Here a very unusual monk carries such patience to an amazing extreme.

There was a certain worldly man who wished to become a monk. He had a little daughter who asked him to take her with him to the monastery. He said, "If you wish to become a nun, let me take you to a house for virgins." But she said to him, "I cannot be separated from you." Her father was greatly distressed because she wept night and day and begged not to be separated from him. He made up his mind to take her with him and changed her name from Maria to Maryana as if she had been a boy. Then he committed the matter to God and took her into a monastery without anyone perceiving that Maryana was a girl. After several years Maryana's father died performing the excellent works of the monastic life. The abbot saw that Maryana was working hard and excelling spiritually and rejoiced in him (not knowing he was not a boy). He commanded that he should not be sent out on the highways to beg because he was a child.

When the abbot saw that the brothers envied Maryana because he did not go out, he called Maryana and said to him, "Since the brothers envy you because you do not do the work as they do, I command you to do it." Then Maryana fell down before the abbot and said, "Whatever you command me to do I will do gladly, O Father." Whenever the brothers went out, they visited a certain believer in order to rest a little and refresh themselves. So when Maryana went out, this believer saw him in the evening and brought him to his house to rest there for the night. The believer had a daughter, and on the night Maryana stayed with him someone seduced her and said, "If your father asks you who seduced you, tell him it was Maryana the monk." As soon as Maryana had departed, the father knew that his daughter had been seduced and asked, "Who has seduced you?" She said, "Maryana, the monk." Then the father immediately went to the monastery and spoke with tears before the abbot and all the brothers, "What offense have I committed against you that you should seduce my daughter?" When the abbot heard this, he was greatly moved and said, "What do you say? Who seduced your daughter? Tell me who it is and I will expel him from the monastery at once." And the man said, "It is Maryana." Then the abbot called for Maryana, but he could not be found. Then they knew that he was out on a journey. The abbot told the father, "There is nothing further I can do but this: when Maryana returns from the highway, I will not allow him to enter."

When Maryana came back from the road, they would not allow him to enter the monastery, and he wept at the door and said, "What is my offense that I am not permitted to enter?" Then the doorkeeper said, "You have seduced the daughter of the believer whom the monks visit." Maryana begged the doorkeeper, "For the Lord's sake go in and persuade the abbot to let me enter the monastery. Whatever he orders because of my fall I will do." So the doorkeeper went in, and the abbot said, "Go tell Maryana, 'Because you have done this, you will never see my face again. Go away wherever you please.'" When Maryana heard that, he was greatly afflicted and sat by the door night and day and wept because of what had happened to him.

After the maiden (through whom Maryana had been trodden in the dust) had given birth to her child, her father took the boy and brought it to Maryana, saying, "Look, here is your son. Take him and raise him." Maryana took the child, saying, "Glory to God who can bear with sinners like myself." Each day he took the child and went up the mountain to the goats of the monastery, and the child nursed on goats' milk. Then Maryana returned to the door of the monastery. He never left the door except when he went to give the child milk. He asked those who went in or out, with tears, to join him in praying God to forgive his sin. He sat there for four years, and tears were never absent from his eyes by night or day. Everyone who heard him weeping was grieved for his sake. For four years Maryana suffered affliction by the door and showed the child to everyone, saying, "Pray for me, for I fell into fornication, and this child is the result of it." Then God moved the abbot's mind to bring Maryana into the monastery.

As soon as Maryana heard this, he fell down before the Lord and said, "Glory to you, O Lord, who have not been unmindful of such a sinner as I am! I thank you for all the goodness you have shown me. What can I give you in return? For you have brought me into the monastery when I thought I must die by the door." Maryana, who was carrying the child and weeping and sighing and groaning, fell down before the abbot and the whole brotherhood and said, "Forgive me, masters and fathers, for I have angered God with evil works and greatly afflicted you. Pray for me, that God may forgive my fall."

After many years Maryana, having prevailed mightily in the great labors of spiritual excellence, delivered his soul to our Lord. When he was dead, the brothers came to anoint him with oil and saw that Maryana was a woman. They ran quickly and called the man who had made the accusation against Maryana. When he came and saw her, great wonder laid hold of him. He begged God to forgive him the great sin and wrong he had done to Maryana.

spiritual direction

From the *Lausiac History of Palladius*

Many people came to the desert fathers seeking a word of direction. In this selection, Macarius, a disciple of Anthony, takes a word to a monk who needs special care.

Abba Macarius used to dwell by himself in the desert. Below him was another desert where many lived. The old man was watching the road one day and saw Satan traveling on it in the form of a man. He was wearing a garment full of holes, and various fruits were hanging about him. The old man Macarius said to him, "Where are you going?" He said, "I am going to visit the brothers and to make them mindful of their work." The old man said, "Why do you need those various fruits?" Satan answered, "I am carrying them to the brothers for food." The old man said, "All these?" And Satan said, "Yes. If one doesn't please a brother, I hand him another. If that doesn't please him, I give him another. One or the other of these must certainly please him." Having said these things, Satan went on his way.

Then the old man kept watching the road until Satan came along to return. When he saw him, he asked, "Have you been successful?" And Satan said, "Where can I get help?" The old man said, "For what purpose?" Satan said, "They have all forsaken me and rebelled against me. Not one of them will allow himself to be persuaded by me." The old man said, "Don't you have even one friend left there?" And Satan said, "Yes, I have one brother, but only one, who will be persuaded by me, even though whenever he sees me, he turns away his face as if from an enemy." The old man said to him, "What is the name of this brother?" And Satan said, "Theopemptus." Then he departed and went on his way.

Abba Macarius rose up and went down to the lower desert. The brothers heard and brought palm leaves and went out to meet him. Every monk prepared his cell, thinking that he would stay there. But the old man asked for the brother named Theopemptus, who received him joyfully. When the brothers began to speak among themselves, the old man said to him, "What do you have to say, my brother? How are your affairs?" And Theopemptus said, "At the present moment matters are well with me," for he was ashamed to speak. The old man said, "Look, I have lived a life of stern discipline for many years and am held in honor by everyone. Nevertheless, even though I am an old man, the spirit of fornication disturbs me." And Theopemptus answered, "Believe me, father, it disturbs me also." And the old man, like one who was bothered by many thoughts, made a reason for talking. At length he led the brother to confess the matter. Afterward, he said to him, "How long do you fast?" The brother said, "Until the ninth hour." The old man said, "Fast until evening and continue to do so. Repeat passages from the book of the Gospels and from the other scriptures. If a thought rises in your mind, don't look downward but always upward, and the Lord will help you." And so, having made the brother reveal his thought and having given him encouragement, he departed to go to his own desert. As he traveled along the road, he watched according to his custom.

He saw the devil again and said to him, "Where are you going?" He answered, "I go to remind the brothers of their work." When he came back again, the holy man said to him, "How are the brothers?" The devil said, "They are in an evil case." And the old man said, "Why?" The devil said, "They are all like savage animals and rebellious. But the worst thing of all is that even the one brother who used to be obedient to me has turned, I know not why. He will not be persuaded by me in any way and is the most savage of them all against me. On account of this, I have taken an oath never again to go to that place or at least only after a very long time."

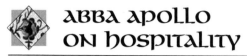

ABBA APOLLO
ON hOSPITALITY

From *History of the Monks in Egypt*

In 394–95, a group of monks from Jerusalem visited Egypt to learn from the desert fathers. One of the party wrote History of the Monks in Egypt, *describing the journey and what they had heard from those they met. In this selection the author tells of the group's reception by Abba Apollo, the leader of a community of five hundred monks.*

When three of us went to visit the blessed Apollo, the brothers with him saw us and recognized us by the descriptions they had heard from him of our journey. They met us with gladness and sang songs of praise, for this is the custom with all the brothers. They bowed down with their faces to the ground, then rose up and gave us the salutation of peace and said to their companions, "Behold, the brothers of whom our abba spoke to us three days ago have come to us." For he had said, "Behold, after three days three brothers will come to you from Jerusalem." Some of the brothers went before us, rejoicing and singing psalms, and some followed behind answering them until we arrived at the place where the blessed man was. When our father Apollo heard the sound of their singing, he also came forth to meet us, according to the custom of the brothers. When he saw us, he was the first to bow

low to the ground. Then he stretched out his hand
and rose up and kissed us and led us in and prayed
and washed our feet with his own hands. He urged us
to rest ourselves and eat, for it was his custom to do
this to all the brothers who came to visit him.

Now the brothers who were with him did not go
straight to their meal, but first received the Eucharist
of Christ together. They did this daily at the ninth
hour and then ate their meal. While they were eating
they learned his commandments until the time for
sleep. Then some of them went into the desert and
repeated the Scriptures by heart the whole night long.
Others stayed with him to glorify God until the
morning. Many of them used to come down at the
ninth hour and receive the Eucharist and then return
to their places. The spiritual food alone would be suf-
ficient for them till the ninth hour on the next day.
Many of them would remain without ordinary food
for several days at a time: from one Sunday to another.
We observed their joy in the desert, with which
nothing on the earth—no bodily delight—can be compared. Among them no one was sorry or afflicted with
grief. But if anyone was found to be in affliction, our
father Apollo knew the cause and was able to tell him
the secret thoughts of his mind. He would say, "It is
not proper for us to be afflicted at our redemption, for
we are those who are about to inherit the kingdom of
heaven. Let evil people be in mourning, and let the
righteous rejoice. For they have their happiness in

earthly things and cultivate them. Why shouldn't we, who are worthy of the blessed hope, rejoice always, according to the encouraging words of the blessed Apostle Paul, 'Rejoice always, pray without ceasing, give thanks in all circumstances'?"

What shall I say concerning the grace in the words of the blessed Apollo? He discussed many things concerning rigorous discipline and exhorted us how to receive the brothers. He told us that when brothers came to visit us, it was proper to bow low before them. "Not," he said, "that we bow down before them, but before God who is in them. When you see your brother, you see Christ. We have derived the custom of urging brothers from time to time to come in and rest and refresh themselves from Abraham and also from Lot, who urged the angels to stay with him.

"If possible, monks should partake of the mysteries of Christ each day. For whoever keeps away from them keeps away from God. For the voice of our Life Giver says, 'Those who eat my flesh and drink my blood abide in me, and I in them.' It is very helpful for monks to remember the passion of our Redeemer at all times because by this remembrance we become worthy of the forgiveness of our sins always. So it is right that we should always make ourselves worthy to receive the holy mysteries of our Redeemer.

"Let no one break the established fasts unless it would cause great suffering. We keep the fast on

Wednesday because on that day the Jews plotted to betray our Lord and on Friday because on that day he was crucified. So whoever breaks these becomes one of the betrayers. But if your brother comes to you during a period of fasting and is in need of refreshment—even at the wrong time—set the table for him by himself. If he does not want to eat, do not force him. This is a universal tradition of hospitality."

On several occasions we conversed together the whole Sabbath. When he was escorting us on our way back, he said to us, "Have peace with one another and let no one separate himself from his companion on the way." Then he said to the brothers who were with him, "Who among you is willing to go and escort these brothers on the way to the other fathers?" With very few exceptions, all the brothers sought anxiously to go with us and to escort us on our way. But the holy man Apollo selected three of them who were mighty in their disciplined work and understanding in their speech. He commanded them not to leave us until we had seen all the fathers whom we wished to see and had rejoiced in conversing with them. Then he blessed us and sent us away, saying, "The Lord bless you from Zion. May you see the prosperity of Jerusalem all the days of your life."

ABBA
PATERMUTHIUS

From *History of the Monks in Egypt*

When the monks visited Abba Copres, he told amazing stories about an earlier monk named Patermuthius.

Patermuthius was first and foremost of all the monks who lived here. He first wore this clothing—he invented it. Formerly he was a thief who plundered the pagan tombs. He had a great reputation for committing wickedness of every kind. He once went to rob the religious house of a certain blessed woman. Without knowing it he found himself on the roof of her house. But he was unable to go into her house and plunder it because the roofs of the house were as flat as the ground and had no rain pipes (there is no rain in Thebaid) and there was no place on the roof to enter the house. So he was neither able to descend nor to escape from it and had to stay there until morning. He wondered meanwhile what to do until daylight came. While he was there he sank into a light sleep and saw an angel who said to him, "Do not devote such close attention and diligence and watching to your life of thievery. If you wish to change your wickedness into a life of good deeds, you must join the army of angels before Christ the King, and you shall receive from him this power and authority." And as soon as he had heard these things, he received them gladly. And the angel showed him a company of monks and commanded that he should lead them.

When he woke up from his slumber, he saw the nun standing before him, saying to him, "O man, what are you doing here? Who are you?" He said, "I do not know, but I beg you to show me the church." When she had shown him the church, he went and fell down before the feet of the elders and entreated them to let him become a Christian so that he might repent. Now when the elders knew who he was, they marveled at him and began to warn him that he must stop being a murderer. He begged them to teach him the Psalms. When he had learned three verses of the first psalm, he said, "These are enough for me to learn." He stayed there three days and then departed into the desert. Patermuthius lived there for three years in prayer and tears and fed himself on the roots in the desert and wandered about eating them.

After three years he returned to the church and repeated before the fathers the belief and all the doctrine of the church. Although he had never learned letters, he could repeat the Scriptures by heart. Then the elders marveled at him and wondered how a man of his kind could have attained such a degree of learning and discipline. When they had baptized him, they entreated him to remain with them. He stayed with them for seven more days, then departed to the desert, where he lived for another seven years. Every

Sunday he found bread in his pillowcloth. When he had prayed and given thanks, he would eat it and then fast again until the following Sunday without any suffering.

He came back again from that wilderness with works of spiritual excellence and demonstrated his rule of abstinence and self-denial and incited many to follow after him. A certain young man asked to become his disciple. Patermuthius received him and dressed him in the way he was dressed: he wore a shirt with short sleeves and an outer garment, and he placed a cowl upon his head and tied a napkin about his loins. He showed him the way and the rules of a life of mourning and trained him and placed a cape on his shoulders.

Now the custom of the blessed man was that when a Christian died, he remained with him the whole night long in vigil and prayer and reverently dressed him and buried him. When that disciple saw him dressing the Christians who died in this way, he said to him, "Will you also dress me in this manner when I die, master?" And he said unto him, "I will dress you in this fashion and wrap you in a shroud until you say to me, 'I have enough.'" Now after no great length of time that disciple died, and the words of his master were indeed fulfilled. Patermuthius dressed him reverently in the fear of God, as was right, and he said in a loud voice before all those who were standing there, "Have I dressed you well, O my son, or do you still lack anything?" And the dead man sent forth a voice, and they all heard it, saying, "You have dressed me, O my father. You have fulfilled your promise and completed your undertaking." Wonder laid hold upon all those who were standing there, and they glorified God. Then the blessed man departed into the desert according to his custom and occupied himself in his daily round of devotion.

ABBA
PAPHNUTIUS

From *History of the Monks in Egypt*

As the monks continued their tour, they were shown the cell of Abba Paphnutius, who had recently died, and learned his story.

After Paphnutius had performed great spiritual deeds, he asked God which of the saints whose lives had been pleasing to God he resembled. An angel appeared to him and said, "You are like a singer who lives in such and such a city." The blessed man made his way to the singer. Having found him, he asked him about his life. The singer answered, "I am a sinner and a miserable wretch and a fornicator. Only a short time ago I gave up a life of theft and became as I am." Paphnutius asked him, "What good have you done?" He answered, "I did not know that I had ever done anything good except once. When I was a thief, I saw a certain holy virgin being forced by thieves. She was nearly raped, but I rescued her from them and took her by night to the city. And on another occasion I found a beautiful woman wandering about in the desert. She had fled from the agents of the general and counselor because of her husband's tax debts. She was crying to herself because of her troubles and because she had to roam about and wander in the desert. When I saw her, I asked her the cause of her weeping. She answered me, 'My lord, ask no questions about a miserable woman like myself. Take me as your slave and carry me wherever you want. My husband owes a debt of three hundred gold coins for taxes to the governor. For the past two years he has been scourged and kept in prison. My three beloved children have been sold into slavery, and I myself have been seized on several occasions and carried off and beaten cruelly. Finally I escaped and fled from place to place. And now I am here wandering about in this desert. For the last three days I have eaten nothing at all.' Then I had compassion on her and took her to my cave and gave her three hundred gold coins. Then I took her to the city so she could free herself and redeem her children and husband."

Then Paphnutius said, "I do not know that I have done anything like this, but you must have heard of my efforts. Now God revealed to me that you were not inferior to me in your works. Since God's care for you is not small, as God has shown me, brother, do not neglect yourself as if you were of no account." And immediately the singer threw away the reed pipe he was holding and abandoned the songs he used to sing to cheer the workers and turned to the sweet words of the Holy Spirit and clung to Paphnutius and departed to the desert. Having passed three years in hard work there, he ended his life with praises and prayers and other works of discipline.

Then he traveled the road of the heavenly beings and was numbered among the company of the holy ones and among the army of the righteous and went to his rest.

Paphnutius asked God again which of the saints he resembled. And again a divine voice came to him: "You are like the chief of a village near you." At once Paphnutius went down there. When he had knocked at the door, the master of the house came, as was his custom, to receive strangers. He opened the door and brought him inside and washed his feet and set a table before him and asked him to eat. The blessed man asked him, "Tell me what good deeds you do, for, according to what God has told me, you are more excellent than many monks." Then the man said, "I am a sinner and not worthy to be compared to monks." The blessed man kept asking him, and the man answered, "I do not feel any urgency to tell you my deeds. But since you have said you were sent by God, I will show you what I have done. For the last thirty years I have kept myself away from my wife and have had intercourse with her only three times. I have three children by her, and they take care of my business. But to this very day I have never stopped receiving strangers. No one in my village can boast of excelling me in hospitality to strangers. No poor person or stranger has ever departed from me with an empty hand or without suitable provisions for the way. I have never neglected to comfort with my gifts the poor person who has been brought low. No strife has ever taken place near me that I have not ended peacefully. The members of my house have never been blamed for committing abominable deeds. I have set my fields aside for everyone's pleasure, and I have gathered in what was left over. I have never allowed the rich to carry away the poor by force. I have never caused anyone to grieve in all my life. I have never passed a bad judgment on anyone. According to the will of God, I know in myself that I have done these things."

When Paphnutius heard the glorious character of the man's life and works, he kissed him on the head and said, "The Lord bless you from Zion. May you see the prosperity of Jerusalem all the days of your life. You have performed these things well, but you are lacking one of the prime virtues: the knowledge of the wisdom of God. You will not be able to acquire that without labor, for you must deny the world and yourself and take up the cross of our Lord and follow him." When that man had heard these things, at once, without consulting his children, he clung to the blessed man and went with him to the mountain.

After three years, Paphnutius saw angels carrying the soul of that man up to heaven and praising God and saying, "Happy are those whom you choose and bring near to live in your courts." And the righteous answered, "Great peace have those who love your law." And Paphnutius knew that that man had filled full his measure.

SAYINGS ON PRAYER

From The Sayings of the Fathers

The wisdom of the desert is preserved in brief stories and sayings as well as longer stories, discourses, and travelers' reports. The Sayings of the Fathers is the greatest collection of these short sayings. Here are several on the general topic of prayer, especially as summarized in the prayer of the tax collector (publican) in Luke 18:13: "God, be merciful to me, a sinner!"

Abba Evagrius said, "Sit in your cell, collecting your thoughts. Remember the day of your death. See then what the death of your body will be; let your spirit be heavy, take pains, condemn the vanity of the world, so as to be able to live always in the peace you have in view without weakening. Remember also what happens in hell and think about the state of the souls down there, their painful silence, their most bitter groanings, their fear, their strife, their waiting. Think of their grief without end and the tears their souls shed eternally. But keep the day of resurrection and of presentation to God in remembrance also. Imagine the fearful and terrible judgment. Consider the fate kept for sinners, their shame before the face of God and the angels and archangels and all people, that is to say, the punishments, the eternal fire, worms that rest not, the darkness, gnashing of teeth, fear, and supplications. Consider also the good things in store for the righteous: confidence in the face of God the Father and God's Son, the angels and archangels and all the people of the saints, the kingdom of heaven, and the gifts of that realm, joy and beatitude.

"Keep in mind the remembrance of these two realities. Weep for the judgment of sinners; afflict yourself for fear lest you too feel those pains. But rejoice and be glad at the lot of the righteous. Strive to obtain those joys but be a stranger to those pains. Whether you be inside or outside your cell, be careful that the remembrance of these things never leaves you so that, thanks to their remembrance, you may at least flee wrong and harmful thoughts."

—

Amma Syncletica said, "Imitate the publican, and you will not be condemned with the Pharisee. Choose the meekness of Moses, and you will find your heart that is a rock changed into a spring of water."

—

Abba Macarius was asked, "How should one pray?" The old man said, "There is no need at all to make long discourses; it is enough to stretch out one's hands and say, 'Lord, as you will, and as you know, have mercy.' And if the conflict grows fiercer, say, 'Lord, help!' God knows very well what we need and shows us mercy."

—

A soldier asked Abba Mius if God accepted repentance. After the old man had taught him many things, he said, "Tell me, my dear, if your cloak is torn, do you throw it away?" He replied, "No, I mend it and use it again." The old man said to him, "If you are so careful about your cloak, will not God be equally careful about God's creature?

—

Amma Sarah said, "If I prayed God that all people should approve of my conduct, I should find myself a penitent at the door of each one, but I shall rather pray that my heart may be pure toward all."

—

Abba Nilus said, "Do not always want everything to turn out as you think it should, but rather as God pleases. Then you will be undisturbed and thankful in your prayer."

—

The blessed Epiphanius, bishop of Cyprus, was told this by the abbot of a monastery that he had in Palestine, "By your prayers we do not neglect our appointed round of psalmody, but we are very careful to recite Terce, Sext, and None." Then Epiphanius corrected them with the following comment, "It is clear that you do not trouble about the other hours of the day, if you cease from prayer. The true monk should have prayer and psalmody continually in his heart."

—

Amma Theodora said, "It is good to live in peace, for the wise person practices perpetual prayer. It is truly a great thing for a virgin or a monk to live in peace, especially for the younger ones. However, you should realize that as soon as you intend to live in peace, at once evil comes and weighs down your soul through depression, faintheartedness, and evil thoughts. It also attacks your body through sickness, debility, weakening of the knees, and all the members. It dissipates the strength of soul and body so that one believes one is ill and no longer able to pray. But if we are vigilant, all these temptations fall away. There was, in fact, a monk who was seized by cold and fever every time he began to pray, and he suffered from headaches too. In this condition, he said to himself, I am ill, and near to death; so now I will get up before I die and pray. By reasoning in this way, he did violence to himself and prayed. When he had finished, the fever abated also. So, by reasoning in this way, the brother resisted and prayed and was able to conquer his thoughts."

—

A brother asked Abba Rufus, "What is interior peace, and what use is it?" The old man said, "Interior peace means to remain sitting in one's cell with fear and knowledge of God, holding far off the remembrance of wrongs suffered and pride of spirit. Such interior peace brings forth all the virtues, preserves the monk from the burning darts of the enemy, and does not allow him to be wounded by them. Yes, brother, acquire it. Keep in mind your future death, remembering that you do not know at what hour the thief will come. Likewise be watchful over your soul."

—

Abba Zeno said, "If a man wants God to hear his prayer quickly, then before he prays for anything else, even his own soul, when he stands and stretches out his hands toward God, he must pray with all his heart for his enemies. Through this action God will hear everything that he asks."

SAYINGS ON
JUDGING OTHERS

From *The Sayings of the Fathers*

It was a constant temptation for those striving to excel in the spiritual life to compare themselves to others. Here are some cautions against passing judgment.

One day Abba Isaac went to a monastery. He saw a brother committing a sin and he condemned him. When he returned to the desert, an angel of the Lord came and stood in front of the door of his cell and said, "I will not let you enter." But he persisted, saying, "What is the matter?" and the angel replied, "God has sent me to ask you where you want to throw the guilty brother whom you have condemned." Immediately he repented and said, "I have sinned; forgive me." Then the angel said, "Get up. God has forgiven you. But from now on, be careful not to judge someone before God has done so."

—

Abba Macarius said, "If you reprove someone, you yourself get carried away by anger and you are satisfying your own passion; do not lose yourself, therefore, in order to save another."

—

A brother at Scetis committed a fault. A council was called to which Abba Moses was invited, but he refused to go to it. Then the priest sent someone to

say to him, "Come, for everyone is waiting for you."
So he got up and went. He took a leaking jug, filled it
with water, and carried it with him. The others came
out to meet him and said to him, "What is this,
Father?" The old man said to them, "My sins run out
behind me, and I do not see them, and today I am
coming to judge the errors of another." When they
heard that, they said no more to the brother but for-
gave him.

—

Whenever Abba Agathon's thoughts urged him
to pass judgment on something that he saw, he would
say to himself, *Agathon, it is not your business to do that.*
Thus his spirit was always recollected.

—

Abba Moses said, "If the monk does not think in
his heart that he is a sinner, God will not hear him."
The brother said, "What does that mean, to think in
his heart that he is a sinner?" Then the old man said,
"When someone is occupied with his own faults, he
does not see those of his neighbor."

—

Abba Nilus said, "Everything you do in revenge
against a brother who has harmed you will come back
to your mind at the time of prayer."

—

It was said of Abba John that when he went to
church at Scetis, he heard some brothers arguing, so
he returned to his cell. He went round it three times

and then went in. Some brothers who had seen him wondered why he had done this, and they went to ask him. He said to them, "My ears were full of that argument, so I circled round in order to purify them, and thus I entered my cell with my mind at rest."

—

A brother asked Abba Poemen, "Is it better to speak or to be silent?" The old man said to him, "One who speaks for God's sake does well; but one who is silent for God's sake also does well."

—

Abba Poemen said, "A man may seem to be silent, but if his heart is condemning others, he is babbling ceaselessly. But there may be another who talks from morning till night and yet he is truly silent. That is, he says nothing that is not profitable."

—

A brother questioned Abba Poemen, saying, "I have found a place where peace is not disturbed by the brothers; do you advise me to live there?" The old man said to him, "The place for you is where you will not harm your brother."

—

Amma Syncletica said, "If you find yourself in a monastery, do not go to another place, for that will harm you a great deal. Just as the bird who abandons the eggs she was sitting on prevents them from hatching, so monks or nuns grow cold and their faith dies when they go from one place to another."

—

A brother asked Abba Poemen, "Some brothers live with me; do you want me to be in charge of them?" The old man said to him, "No, just work first and foremost, and if they want to live like you, they will see to it themselves." The brother said to him, "But it is they themselves, Father, who want me to be in charge of them." The old man said to him, "No, be their example, not their legislator."

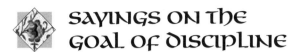

SAYINGS ON THE GOAL OF DISCIPLINE

From *The Sayings of the Fathers*

In many ways, the men and women of the desert were asked, "What should I do?" or "What is this life really about?" Here are some of the answers.

Abba John said, "I think it best that a person should have a little bit of all the virtues. Therefore, get up early every day and acquire the beginning of every virtue and every commandment of God. Use great patience, with fear and long-suffering, in the love of God, with all the fervor of your soul and body. Exercise great humility; bear with interior distress; be vigilant and pray often with reverence and groaning, with purity of speech and control of your eyes. When you are despised, do not get angry; be at peace, and do not render evil for evil. Do not pay attention to the faults of others, and do not try to compare yourself with others, knowing you are less than every created thing. Renounce everything material and what is of the flesh. Live by the Cross, in warfare, in poverty of spirit, in voluntary spiritual asceticism, in fasting, penitence, and tears, in discernment, in purity of soul, taking hold of what is good. Do your work in peace. Persevere in keeping vigil, in hunger and thirst, in cold and nakedness, and in sufferings. Shut yourself in a tomb as though you were already dead so that at all times you will think death is near."

—

A brother questioned an old man, saying, "What good work should I do so that I may live?" The old man said, "God knows what is good. I have heard it said that one of the fathers asked Abba Nisterus the Great, the friend of Abba Anthony, and said to him, 'What good work is there that I could do?' He said to him, 'Are not all actions equal? Scripture says that Abraham was hospitable and God was with him. David was humble, and God was with him. Elias loved interior peace, and God was with him. So, do whatever you see your soul desires according to God and guard your heart.'"

—

A brother asked Abba Poemen what he should do about his sins. The old man said to him, "Those who wish to purify their faults purify them with tears, and those who wish to acquire virtues acquire them with tears. For weeping is the way the Scriptures and our fathers give us when they say 'Weep!' Truly, there is no other way than this."

—

A brother questioned Abba Matoes, saying, "Give me a word." He said to him, "Go, and pray God to put compunction in your heart and give you humility; be aware of your faults; do not judge others but put yourself below everyone; do not be friendly with a boy or with a heretical friend; put freedom of speech far from you; control your tongue and your belly; drink only a small quantity of wine; and if someone speaks about some topic, do not argue with him, but if he is right, say, 'Yes'; if he is wrong, say, 'You know what you are saying,' and do not argue with him about what he has said. That is humility."

—

Abba Poemen said, "To throw yourself before God, not to measure your progress, to leave behind all self-will—these are the instruments for the work of the soul."

—

Abba Poemen said, "If three people meet, of whom the first fully preserves interior peace, and the second gives thanks to God in illness, and the third serves with a pure mind, these three are doing the same work."

—

Someone asked Abba Anthony, "What must one do in order to please God?" The old man replied, "Pay attention to what I tell you: whoever you may be, always have God before your eyes; whatever you do, do it according to the testimony of the Holy Scriptures; in whatever place you live, do not easily leave it. Keep these three precepts and you will be saved."

—

Abba Poemen said that Abba John said that the saints are like a group of trees, each bearing different fruit, but watered from the same source. The practices of one saint differ from those of another, but the same Spirit works in all of them.

—

Amma Syncletica said, "In the beginning there are a great many battles and a good deal of suffering for those who are advancing toward God and afterward, ineffable joy. It is like those who wish to light a fire; at first they are choked by the smoke and cry, and by this means obtain what they seek (as it is said: 'Our God is a consuming fire'): so we also must kindle the divine fire in ourselves through tears and hard work."

—

Abba Amoun of Nitria came to see Abba Anthony and said to him, "Since my rule is stricter than yours, how is it that your name is better known among people than mine is?" Abba Anthony answered, "It is because I love God more than you."

—

Abba Lot went to see Abba Joseph and said to him, "Abba, as far as I can, I say my little office; I fast a little; I pray and meditate; I live in peace; and as far as I can, I purify my thoughts. What else can I do?" Then the old man stood up and stretched his hands toward heaven. His fingers became like ten lamps of fire, and he said to him, "If you will, you can become all flame."

appendix

Reading Spiritual Classics for Personal and Group Formation

Many Christians today are searching for more spiritual depth, for something more than simply being good church members. That quest may send them to the spiritual practices of New Age movements or of Eastern religions such as Zen Buddhism. Christians, though, have their own long spiritual tradition, a tradition rich with wisdom, variety, and depth.

The great spiritual classics testify to that depth. They do not concern themselves with mystical flights for a spiritual elite. Rather, they contain very practical advice and insights that can support and shape the spiritual growth of any Christian. We can all benefit by sitting at the feet of the masters (both male and female) of Christian spirituality.

Reading spiritual classics is different from most of the reading we do. We have learned to read to master a text and extract information from it. We tend to read quickly, to get through a text. And we summarize as we read, seeking the main point. In reading spiritual classics, though, we allow the text to master and form us. Such formative reading goes more slowly, more reflectively, allowing time for God to speak to us through the text. God's word for us may come as easily from a minor point or even an aside as from the major point.

Formative reading requires that you approach the text in humility. Read as a seeker, not an expert. Don't demand that the text meet your expectations for what an "enlightened" author should write. Humility means accepting the author as another imperfect human, a product of his or her own time and situation. Learn to celebrate what is foundational in an author's writing without being overly disturbed by what is peculiar to the author's life and times. Trust the text as a gift from both God and the author, offered to you for your benefit — to help you grow in Christ.

To read formatively, you must also slow down. Feel free to reread a passage that seems to speak specially to you. Stop from time to time to reflect on what you have been reading. Keep a journal for these reflections. Often the act of writing can itself prompt further, deeper reflection. Keep your notebook open and your pencil in hand as you read. You might not get back to that wonderful insight later. Don't worry that you are not getting through an entire passage — or even the first paragraph! Formative reading is about depth rather than breadth, quality rather than quantity. As you read, seek God's direction for your own life. Timeless truths have their place but may not be what is most important for your own formation here and now.

As you read the passage, you might keep some of these questions running through your mind:

- How is what I'm reading true of my own life? Where does it reflect my own *experience*?

- How does this text challenge me? What new *direction* does it offer me?

- What must I change to put what I am reading into practice? How can I *incarnate* it, let this word become flesh in my life?

You might also devote special attention to sections that upset you. What is the source of the disturbance? Do you want to argue theology? Are you turned off by cultural differences? Or have you been skewered by an insight that would turn your life upside down if you took it seriously? Let your journal be a dialogue with the text.

If you find yourself moving from reading the text to chewing over its implications to praying, that's great! Spiritual reading is really the first step in an ancient way of prayer called *lectio divina* or "divine reading." Reading leads naturally into reflection on what you have read (meditation). As you reflect on what the text might mean for your life, you may well want to ask for God's help in living out any new insights or direction you have perceived (prayer). Sometimes such prayer may lead you further into silently abiding in God's presence (contemplation). And, of course, the process is only really completed when it begins to make a difference in the way we live (incarnation).

As good as it is to read spiritual classics in solitude, it is even better to join with others in a small group for mutual formation or "spiritual direction in common." This is *not* the same as a study group that talks about spiritual classics. A group for mutual formation would have similar goals as for an individual's reading: to allow the text to shine its light on the *experiences* of the group members, to suggest new *directions* for their lives and practical ways of *incarnating* these directions. Such a group might agree to focus on one short passage from a classic at each meeting (even if members have read more). Discussion usually goes much deeper if all the members have already read and reflected on the passage before the meeting and bring their journals.

Such groups need to watch for several potential problems. It is easy to go off on a tangent (especially if it takes the focus off the members' own experience and onto generalities). At such times a group leader might bring the group's attention back to the text: "What does our author say about that?" Or, "How do we experience that in our own lives?" When a group member shares a problem, others may be tempted to try to "fix" it. This is much less helpful than sharing similar experiences and how they were handled (for good or ill). "Sharing" someone else's problems (whether that person is in or out of the group) should be strongly discouraged.

One person could be designated as leader, to be responsible for opening and closing prayers; to be the first to share or respond to the text; and to keep notes during the discussion to highlight recurring themes, challenges, directives, or practical steps. These responsibilities could also be shared among several members of the group or rotated.

For further information about formative reading of spiritual classics, try *A Practical Guide to Spiritual Reading* by Susan Annette Muto. *Shaped by the Word* by Robert Mulholland (Upper Room Books®) covers formative reading of the Bible. *Good Things Happen: Experiencing Community in Small Groups* by Dick Westley is an excellent resource on forming small groups of all kinds.